CRIME AND PUZZLEMENT 5

ON MARTHA'S VINEYARD, MOSTLY

CRIME AND Puzzlement 5

ON MARTHA'S VINEYARD, MOSTLY

24 SOLVE-THEM-YOURSELF PICTURE MYSTERIES

Lawrence Treat

ILLUSTRATED BY PAUL KARASIK

AN OWL BOOK • HENRY HOLT AND COMPANY

NEW YORK

Henry Holt and Company, Inc.
Publishers since 1866
115 West 18th Street
New York, New York 10011

Henry Holt® is a registered trademark
of Henry Holt and Company, Inc.

Library of Congress Catalog Card Number: 93-078100

ISBN 0-8050-1593-0 (An Owl Book: pbk.)

Henry Holt books are available for special promotions
and premiums. For details contact: Director, Special Markets.

First Edition—1993

Designed by Lucy Albanese

Printed in the United States of America
All first editions are printed on acid-free paper.∞

10 9 8 7 6 5 4

CONTENTS

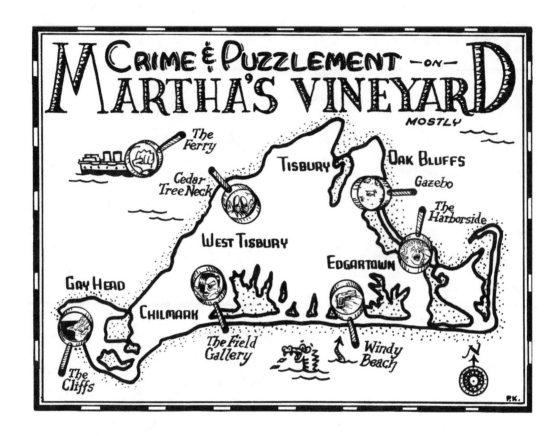

INTRODUCTION

Let me first make it clear that all the cases described in this book are authentic and recorded in official files, which somehow disappeared—a fact that proves they are genuine. Why else would they disappear?

Most of the cases happened on Martha's Vineyard, an island off the coast of Massachusetts. Whaling was once the Vineyard's main industry, but today it is known as a vacation paradise, with a population that burgeons from about 15,000 in winter to perhaps 90,000 in summer.

Gay Head, at the southwestern end of the island, is run largely by the Wampanoag tribe. In contrast to this rural setting, the three "down island" towns have most of the shops, supermarkets, restaurants, and movies—of which there is one every weekend during the winter.

The island is fiercely independent, and a few years ago it tried to secede from the United States. It got as far as designing its own flag and composing its own national anthem, and then ran out of gas.

The six island towns have six different governments, six zoning boards, six libraries, five grade schools, six fire departments, and one regional high school. Four of the six towns are dry. As for a regional police department—well, ask Sam about that.

I first met Sam on Menemsha Beach on one of those mythical summer days when children are models of obedience, traffic is sparse, and you can walk into the Black Dog Tavern around seven in the evening and find an empty table on the porch. Reality, however, is somewhat different, and the island is not without crime—nor without ticks or poison ivy or rainy days—and a crime rate, which were it not for Sam would be unacceptable.

Everybody knows him. He's a kindly looking man who needs three or four inches of height before he can even think of playing basketball—which he doesn't want to bother with anyway. His overwhelming interest is in crime and the prevention of it. So dedicated is he to his profession, he's been known to ferret out crime even when it doesn't exist, which leaves him mildly embarrassed but chuckling to himself. (It is worth noting that the chuckle is out of date. People laugh, titter, smile, or hee-haw, but only a few have cultivated the gentle art of the chuckle—Sam is one of them.)

Sam prefers not to be recognized or addressed as Chief of Martha's Vineyard All-Island Regional Police Department, which doesn't even exist. But will, as soon as they agree on where to meet. Which they will, as soon as . . .

It's obvious that Sam has a rare talent for being at the right place at the right time. But knowing him as I do, I can attest that he has no "right" abilities other than the basic ones of observation and logic, which are all you need to solve, for instance, the case of the Awesome Treasure, or to deal with the Great "Drug" Bust, or the serious matter of the Kippered Herrings.

Sam had no trouble with any of the above. Although born an islander, he started his career on the mainland, and I've included a couple of his early cases, like the raucous affair of those pesky ghouls and goblins. And I've recorded the time he went off-island to Mudville and saw the mighty Casey slide home in a cloud of dust. (Even though that one was not Sam's case, it shows his levelheadedness in crisis and his use of plain, ordinary common sense. Same as you have, which is why you bought this book in the first place.)

So, read the text carefully, study the expert drawings by long-time Vineyarder Paul Karasik, and then go ahead and solve these puzzles. Oh, in case one or two of these should stymie you (or if you just don't feel like bothering to be a sleuth), then look in the back of the book and cheat.

But don't let Sam find out.

How to Solve the Puzzles

1. Always read the narrative first. It supplies you with vital clues.

2. Read all the questions through without trying to answer them. This will give you a sense of what to look for in the picture.

3. Examine the picture.

4. Grab your pencil.

5. Answer the questions, one at a time and in order. If you're a beginner, it might help if you check your answers as you go along to make sure that you're on the right track. Once you think your detecting skills are sharp enough, you may want to skip the preliminary questions altogether and go straight for the big one at the end.

6. Look at the solution and either congratulate yourself on a job well done or resolve to do better next time. Then move on to the next puzzle.

CRIME AND PUZZLEMENT 5

ON MARTHA'S VINEYARD, MOSTLY

BANG, BANG!

Sam loved crowds and never missed the Sunday evenings when the high school band performed in the gazebo in the center of Ocean Park, an open area in Oak Bluffs that borders on the Vineyard Sound.

He was there on a Sunday evening in August when, as usual, people came in droves and picnicked on the lawn. Some of them had to park almost a mile away, and they came as much for the music as for the spectacle of the audience flocking down to the bandstand, which they circled in a parade of dancing and prancing and whooping it up. It was routine for Sam to have a few police available whenever there was a crowd.

Standing on the outskirts of the park, he was hoping to spot the men who, in the course of a burglary the previous night, had jumped from a second-floor balcony and escaped with a haul of jewelry. Shortly after the break-in, a man calling himself J. Rolf hobbled into the emergency room of Martha's Vineyard Hospital. His leg was subsequently put in a cast, after which he commandeered a wheelchair and disappeared, presumably with the help of an accomplice. Thus far, the pair were still at liberty.

The band was working up to a crescendo of drums and brasses and the final crash of cymbals when the cymbalist overcymbaled and lost control of one of his discs. It went flying and hit a tall bearded man on the shoulder. He had been pushing a wheelchair labeled MVH, but with the blow, he tripped and the occupant was catapulted from his seat and sent sprawling on the grass. In the semidarkness the bearded man fled.

It took Sam a minute to shoulder through the knot of people staring down at a man with a cast on his leg and a bullet hole in his chest. The body had been stripped of all objects that could identify it.

Meanwhile, the police arrested two bearded men who resembled each other, each of whom was accused of being the man who had been pushing the wheelchair. Both men declined the honor of being questioned by Sam, but nevertheless acquiesced when Sam asked to see the contents of their pockets. The total contents of each man's pockets were separately labeled for evidence, one man's as A and the other's as B. After examining A and B carefully, Sam made an arrest.

Which of the two men did Sam charge, and on what counts?

Questions

1. Was the dead man one of the burglars?

2. What are two possible reasons for his being killed?

3. Was he killed in the immediate vicinity of Ocean Park?

4. Why was the body put in a wheelchair?

5. What was Sam's reasoning, and what charges did he make?

Solution on page 51.

WINDY BEACH

Sam is a dedicated windsurfer, and his bright red sail with the oversized lettering (embroidered by Officer Nancy Nashawena) had been featured in the local *Gazette*, so it's obvious that everybody would recognize him and his board.

He was surfing off a windy stretch of beach (and had admittedly gone much farther out than he should have) when he heard a shot. For a moment he didn't know where it came from, but as he rounded a small promontory, he saw three or four people on the beach. Two of them were locked in a struggle. As Sam watched, they both fell, but before he could see anything else through the salt-encrusted window of his sail, a gust of wind caught him and sent him floundering into the sea.

In the rough, wind-driven waters, it took him some time before he managed to climb upon his board again and head for land. There, he saw what you see. After ascertaining that the man was dead and had been shot at close range, Sam expected a routine arrest.

A heavyset bald man standing nearby disillusioned him.

"I'm Toby Ecclestrip," he said. "This is my private beach, and I'll save you the trouble of digging up information which you'll obtain anyhow.

"This is my wife, known as 'Sexy Suzie,'" he said, pointing to her. Whereupon Suzie gave a smile and a corroborative wriggle. Ecclestrip then pointed to a man standing nearby. "And this is my colleague, Roderick Soothsayer. We have a business in which we forecast what your life will be after you've been reincarnated. Manuel Terwilliger, a client freshly deceased [and Ecclestrip indicated the corpse] was suing us for five million because he wanted to be rich in his next life and we told him he couldn't be, so we arranged to meet here and discuss the matter amicably. Instead, he made impossible demands and tried to enforce them at gun point. *His* gun, of course. Roddy tried to stop him, and in their struggle Terwilliger's gun went off and killed him."

Soothsayer objected. "Toby's account has one inaccuracy. He, not me, had the fight. I was merely a witness."

Sam listened attentively, examined the terrain, and asked Soothsayer how old he was. Soothsayer said he was twenty-two, whereupon Sam made his arrest.

Whom did he charge, and why?

Questions

1. Had Terwilliger brought the gun that killed him?

2. Did Ecclestrip and Soothsayer have motives for killing Terwilliger?

3. Do you think that Terwilliger's body would have been left on the beach if Sam had not appeared so fortuitously?

4. Can you tell whose footsteps led to the area where the fight or scuffle took place?

5. Who shot Terwilliger?

Solution on page 51.

STRADEGY

The ululations of the Belle, Belle, Belle brought the neighbors running (they're a friendly lot) to the small practice studio of the violinist Nicolo Pagachini. There they found what you see in the sketch. Pagachini was apparently dead from a blow on the head, and his wife, Belle, seemed inconsolable.

Sam learned that Paggy (as his friends called him) had suffered a stroke a couple of months ago, and although he was recovering, his musical career was definitely over. Belle stopped ululating long enough to tell Sam that Paggy's violin was an authentic Stradivarius insured for several million dollars and that an insurance agent named Harold Bolen had been due this very afternoon to examine it and—they hoped—appraise it at a higher value.

To complicate matters, Sam also found out that Paggy's brother-in-law, Tomasino Smith, was an amateur musician who craved the Strad and wanted to buy it, and buy it cheap. Both Harold and Tomasino had been in the vicinity of the studio shortly before Belle had set to her wailing.

Whom did Sam accuse of killing Paggy, and why?

Questions

1. Had there been a fight?

2. Did Paggy use his Strad to defend himself?

3. Were the furniture and other objects broken during the course of a fight?

4. Do you think that the Strad was worth top value before the fight?

5. Who killed Pagachini?

Solution on page 52.

THE PEEK-A-BOO GIRL

The Field Gallery in West Tisbury is a simple geometrical structure of weather-beaten pine. But outside on a two-acre lawn Tom Maley has created a whimsical group of sculptured nymphs and goddesses and fauns. Here tourists have their pictures taken, weddings take place, and an occasional Shakespearean play is performed.

One Friday morning in late August, four people, entranced by this array of sculpture, were waiting for the gallery to open. At ten A.M. sharp, Fanny Bright, in charge of the gallery, got up from her desk and opened the doors. Ten minutes later the four came running at her with the news that *The Peek-a-Boo Girl,* a controversial work that had been touring the country, was slashed.

The four people were: Jose Gonza, a psychiatrist from Guatemala; Wendy Wurry, a patient under his care; Sydney Walstreet, owner of the Walstreet Gallery; and Jay Walker, an artist who was showing at the Walstreet Gallery and not drawing much of a crowd.

Fanny called Sam immediately. It was routine procedure to search Fanny and the four visitors and then make a thorough search of the premises. When nothing turned up, Sam went about questioning his suspects. Jose said he'd walked into the main room from one of its two entrances and seen Walstreet and Walker standing in front of the painting and talking quietly. Wendy said she'd come in from the other entrance and also had seen Walstreet and Walker talking. Sydney and Jay admitted it and said they'd been shocked at the vandalism and were discussing the extent of the damage when the two others came in. They all got excited at the damage, and all four went to report the matter to Fanny.

While Sam was evaluating the various statements, Wendy suddenly began screaming hysterically and pointing to Fanny.

"She—she did it! I know because I'm psychic. She used an old stiletto and it's in her drawer right now!"

Fanny was astounded. "She's obviously crazy, making such wild accusations." Then Fanny gave a shrug. "Go ahead and find it," she said to Wendy.

Wendy, still in a frenzy, gave Fanny a violent shove and elbowed her way past. "See!" she said, yanking open the drawer. "Look in here!"

The sketch shows both *The Peek-a-Boo Girl* and the drawer of Fanny's desk, with all the objects in it. Sam, not moving, studied the contents of the drawer, then stepped back and nodded.

What did he notice, and whom did he then take into custody?

Questions

1. Did Walker have a motive for sabotage?

2. Did Walstreet have a motive for sabotage?

3. Could one of the four have gone straight to the picture, slashed it, and, returning later on, pretend to discover the sabotage?

4. Are Walker's and Walstreet's accounts credible?

5. Can you think of a hiding place that Sam obviously missed?

6. Who slashed the picture?

Solution on page 53.

TREAD LIGHTLY

Grinny Jerome appeared on the island every July and left promptly on Labor Day. In the interval she slept wherever there was a roof, and she ate mostly from the refreshment tables at gallery openings, of which there are many. Occasionally, when pickings were lean, she broke into a house and stole some food, usually sweets.

Sam hated to arrest her for raiding a cookie jar, but he wished he had when Melissa Kindly went looking for mushrooms in the Felix Neck Wildlife Sanctuary and instead of finding *Pluteus umbrosis,* she found a body. It turned out to be that of Grinny. She was killed by a single bullet, and the gun, never traced, lay next to her.

Because Melissa immediately went for help and disturbed nothing, the probable time of death was established, and Sam was able to photograph the nearby shoe prints, as shown. They were particularly clear in the muddy area where a few planks had been left as part of a nature trail.

Sam's investigation moved swiftly. His first step was to locate the abandoned shack where Grinny had been living. There he found a change of clothes and $800 in new twenty-dollar bills. His next step was to learn that one of the Sperlings had withdrawn $800 in new twenty-dollar bills.

Sam was aware that Noah Sperling, known as the Moped King, operated his business with his three sons—Abel, the oldest, and the twins, Babel and Cabel—and that the business was usually in violation of some kind of regulation.

Sam tried to question Noah, but Noah said, "I don't shoot women," and kicked Sam out of his office.

Abel was more amenable. Despite a recent moped accident that left him hobbling around on crutches, he'd been seen near the Felix Neck headquarters on the afternoon of the murder. He admitted being there for a few minutes, but claimed he'd been in Gay Head the rest of the afternoon. As for the twins, Babel said he and Cabel had gone fishing, and Cabel backed him up with identical details.

Sam, armed with a photograph of the footprints and officer Pudge Bartlett to back him up in case of trouble, asked permission to examine the shoes of all four Sperlings. When nobody objected, Sam made his search and found a single mud-encrusted sneaker that matched the prints in the swamp. The shoe was Abel's, and pointed to his good foot.

Instead of asking further questions, Sam made his arrest on the spot.

Whom did he arrest, and how did he figure things out?

Questions

1. Do you think that Grinny was black-mailing Abel Sperling?

2. Do you think that any of the alibis have merit?

3. Does Abel's shoe print constitute enough evidence to hold him for further questioning?

4. Does Abel's acquiescence to the search tend to clear him or implicate him, or neither?

5. Whom did Sam arrest, and on what basis?

Solution on page 53.

A MATTER OF DELICACY

William Makepiece Thatchery, known as "Willy," and his wife, Louise, known as "The Lulu," were nervous about the private, expensively catered luncheon that they were about to give in their Edgartown home. As disinterested parties they hoped to effect a *rapprochement* between the ambassador of...well, let's not say where, because a certain touchy situation had arisen and the ambassador had enemies, which was why he was forced to the secrecy of this luncheon meeting with the foreign minister of...best not to mention who because there had been threats, and if it became known that he was negotiating with the foreign minister of...well, there would be repercussions.

Suffice it to say that Willy and The Lulu were worried about the whole business and had decided that the wine they chose would be crucial. After all, a good wine makes for a good bargain. They therefore set out hand in hand (a habit inherited from both their families) determined to buy a wine worthy of the occasion. Luckily, they were able to find an '86 Oceanus, a rare wine produced in small quantities by the local Chicama Vineyard.

Before going, The Lulu checked on the table setting to make sure it was adequate. Later, when she and Willy returned, each of them carrying one of the precious bottles, she was jubilant, but not Willy. He had a photographic memory, and he frowned as he studied the room. Recalling it in detail, he noted six differences. Then, visibly annoyed, he uttered one word.

What was the word he uttered, what were the differences he noted, and what did he do about it?

Questions

1. Had any of the dishes been stolen?

2. Had any of the silverware been stolen?

3. Aside from the dishes and silverware, what objects have been tampered with?

4. Was burglary the motive for the intrusion?

5. What was the word Willy uttered?

Solution on page 54.

In All That Rain

One rainy day the body of Hairy Harry Hearrowitch (pronounced "Harch") was found on a lonely dirt road about a mile from his house in Vineyard Haven. The body was reeking of alcohol, and it seemed clear that Harry either fell or was pushed into the puddle. Sam, studying the body, found no wound.

Sam knew Harry as an antique dealer who'd been accused of faking some of his best items, with the result that there were plenty of people who might have killed him—if he'd been killed. At the head of the list was his wife, Elsbeth, whom he beat regularly, as per a schedule posted in the kitchen. Next came his partner, Calvin Sackett, with whom he quarreled frequently. And finally there was Jughead Piker, whom Harry chased out of the house whenever he caught him with Elsbeth.

Sam, with all of the above in his head, went to Harry's. After noting that Harry's car was in the driveway, he proceeded to interview Elsbeth. She told him that this morning Harry had had $5,000 in cash, which, according to Elsbeth, he intended to use to pay Sackett to cancel a personal loan that had just come due.

"Poor Harry!" she said. "He loved to walk in the rain and he must have gotten mugged and then left there on the road. Robbed and murdered—what an end!"

Sam, however, was less than sympathetic and suggested that Elsbeth might have wanted to get back at Harry for all the years of abuse.

She seemed shocked at the idea. "Why would I do that now?" she demanded. "Just look at me—all week long and not even a black eye!"

As for Sackett, he showed Sam an IOU with Harry's signature. "I expected him to come here with the money, but he never showed up."

Sam talked the case over with a couple of his officers and came to a conclusion. What do you think it was, and why?

Questions

1. Do you think that Harry went walking in the rain?

2. Why was the car in the driveway?

3. Did Sackett lie?

4. What did Sam conclude, and what did he do about it?

Solution on page 54.

Of Ghouls and Goblins

Algernon Meany, a small man in a small off-island town, was hated by many and loved by none. He had recently bought an old-fashioned vaudeville troupe and immediately fired half the players and cut everyone else's salary by 40 percent.

On Hallowe'en, when he gave a party to all children under the age of nine, he was temporarily forgiven his sins. The affair was held in the Community Center. Adults had to wait outside, while kids were screened at the door and given masks of ghouls and goblins and incubi. Naturally, Meany took over the stage himself, chiefly to show off his line of new toys, which was the main purpose of the evening.

The event ended spectacularly, in a burst of firecrackers and a blinding blaze of light, at which time Meany stepped forward and proclaimed himself King of All Toyland. Dramatic to the end, he was shot in the middle of his finale and fell with an unearthly screech that scared the kids into a panic and sent them rushing into the waiting arms of their parents.

Sam, who happened to be present as the colleague of Amos Kerplunk, the Deputy Chief of Police, was immediately pressed into service and agreed that the empty jack-in-the-box was too small to hold even a child. Thoughtfully, Sam looked on as Kerplunk found the murder weapon underneath a chair near the front of the hall, as shown.

Kerplunk, in a hoarse voice that scared children into immediate submission, rounded up the ones who had been sitting near the gun and questioned them one by one—or tried to.

He started out with Amy Fanz. According to her, Billy Jones had sat in the chair under which the gun was found, but Billy interrupted her to say he hadn't been anywhere near there, and Henry Maxim backed him up, but Henry Hopkins disagreed and said Henry Andrews had sat there, but Milly Perkins claimed that was where she'd sat, only Sylvie Marsh called her a liar, and one of the Henrys said James Finney had sat there, only Henry said James hadn't even been in the theater, and James, who hadn't been there, backed her up, but Amy interrupted to say...

At that point, Kerplunk gave up and turned the whole investigation over to Sam. Sam thanked all the children and told them to go home. With Kerplunk wondering what Sam had in mind, he followed Sam to Meany's nearby office. After studying the names and specialties of everyone in the vaudeville troupe, Sam told Kerplunk whom to arrest.

Whom did Sam accuse, and why?

Questions

1. Could the shot have gone unnoticed in the confusion of noise and lights?

2. Could a seven-year-old have fired the gun?

3. What did Sam see on the stage that sent him to Meany's office?

4. Whom did Sam accuse of killing Meany?

Solution on page 55.

CASEY AT THE PLATE

W hen the mighty Casey took that desperate ninth-inning slide at home plate and was called out, leaving the Martha's Vineyard Nine as the undisputed champions, the Mudville Pies fans erupted with cries of "Kill the ump! Bump the chump!" The umpire in question, I. M. Fair, managed to disappear immediately after the game. As for Casey, he sneaked off in disgrace.

For the next few hours, the Mudville bars were crowded and the mob ran rampant, ending up in a riot at the hotel where I. M. and his wife were thought to be hiding.

Furniture was smashed and several rooms were vandalized, but I. M. was no longer there. According to his account, he had escaped by climbing down a rain spout. He said he hated to leave "The Lady," as he called his wife, but after locking the door and warning her to open it to no one except himself, he left, saying he'd be back in a couple of hours. When he phoned her later, however, he was unable to reach her through the hotel switchboard, and he asked the clerk to go up to her room. The clerk, Twinky Starr, found the door open and The Lady's body lying in the bedroom, as shown.

When Mudville Police Chief Valerie Keen suggested that Sam team up with her in the investigation, he jumped at the chance. (He has since regarded the case as one of his own.)

After viewing the scene, the two chiefs questioned Twinky, the umpire, and the only other people known to have gone up to the second floor, where the Fairs had been staying in room 209. They were: Twinky Starr, the clerk; Sports Winnegar, manager of the Mudville Pies; Slippery Helm, his friend and long-time advisor; and Eric the Dead, so-called because he was usually dead-drunk.

Twinky, still reeling under the shock of finding a dead body, admitted telling Sports the number of the Fair room but swore she'd never left her post at the desk except for her brief visit to 209. Eric, however, said he'd seen her come out of the Fair suite. Asked how he knew it was I. M.'s room, Eric grew confused and asked for another drink.

On the basis of the above facts and statements, and after a careful examination of the bedroom, the two chiefs sized up the situation and made their diagnosis, after which Valerie made her arrest.

Whom did she arrest?

Questions

1. Do you think that the suspects could have transferred their hatred of the umpire to his wife?

2. Do you think that The Lady unlocked the room after I. M. had left?

3. Is it believable that when the clerk told Sports the Fair room number, she also gave him a pass key?

4. Had the bedroom been ransacked?

5. What is the evidence against Sports Winnegar? Against Slippery Helm? Against Twinky Starr? Against Eric the Dead? Against I. M. Fair himself?

6. Whom did Valerie arrest?

Solution on page 55.

A COMEDY OF ERRORS

Sam loved kids and figured the more time he spent with them, the less crime there would be on the island. One of his favorite games was to hand out copies of a drawing with a known number of mistakes and challenge the class to find all of them. When they protested that the test was so hard that he himself wouldn't have been able to pass it, he challenged them to give him a drawing with a known number of mistakes and see if he could find all of them.

They accepted the challenge. After a week of figuring out a tough one, they handed him the drawing shown here. He studied it for about five minutes before returning it with a list of the mistakes he'd found.

"Thirteen," he said. "What mark do I get?"

The class was divided. Half of them wanted to give him a mark of 100%, the other half voted for an A+.

How many can you find?

Solution on page 56.

Missy Takes a Walk

Obed Dagget Road is a steep, stony trail that leads downhill to the parking lot at the Cedar Tree Neck Sanctuary. Officer Nancy Mayhew happened to be in the lot when she was notified of a body apparently strangled and lying on the far side of the small creek that runs parallel to the Yellow Trail, one of the four marked in color for hikers in the preserve. She immediately blocked off the road with her car and called Sam. Then, with nine-year-old Timmy Rattigan, who had discovered the body, she proceeded to the scene, which is shown.

On the way, Timmy told her how he'd left his parents behind and climbed up the embankment. At first, all he'd seen were two feet sticking out from a pile of branches, which he pushed aside.

"And then," he said, "you know what?"

Nancy knew. Standing on the Yellow Trail and surveying the glade on the left side of the creek, she noted the poison ivy and decided to tell Timmy's mother to get him home fast and wash him with hot water and brown soap, and do it good.

Sam arrived promptly, checked the cars, and was able to identify the victim as Missy Moreno, a devout bird-watcher from Oklahoma. She'd apparently been strangled with a scarf, presumably her own.

Sam returned to the parking lot and was waiting for the ambulance when three hikers showed up. They identified themselves as the Apollo brothers—Tony, a mason; Joe, a truck driver; and Ricco, an out-of-work fireman. All three denied any knowledge of the homicide and claimed they'd been together on the Blue Trail, every single instant that afternoon. Questioned in detail as to precisely where they'd been, they were vague and gave conflicting accounts.

"Trees," Joe said. "Nothing but trees around. What's different about a tree?"

On the basis of the above facts, plus an examination of the scene, Sam made an arrest. Whom did he arrest, and why?

Questions

1. How did the camera reach its present position?

2. How did the tripod and Missy's other possessions reach their present position?

3. On which side of the stream had Missy been photographing?

4. On which side of the stream had Missy been killed?

5. How did the makeshift bridge break?

6. How had Missy reached the glade where her body was found?

7. Who killed Missy?

Solution on page 57.

BUCK SHOT

One memorable winter, all six island towns buzzed with the story of the feud between Buck Thorne and Knut Knudsen, both of whom claimed lobstering rights in the same area and were raiding each other's pots. The trouble reached a climax one evening when Sam and Officer Walt Hanna, patrolling Circuit Avenue, heard two shots. Startled, they raced off in the general direction from which they figured the shots had come.

They were lucky, and at the tennis courts on Wamsutta Avenue, they found a small crowd that had just come out of the nearby Oak Bluffs Senior Center. Near the courts and about fifty feet apart were two cars. Knut Knudsen was standing next to one and was apparently trying to explain what had happened. The other car held the body of Buck Thorne.

Sam, leaving procedural details to Hanna, noticed that one shot had entered through the car door window, killing Buck, while a second shot, apparently fired by Buck, had exited through the window. With this in mind, Sam gave his full attention to Knut.

According to Knut, he'd arrived first. When Buck drove up, Knut got out of his car, expecting Buck to do the same, but instead, Buck shot at him.

"He missed," Knut said. "I shot back in self-defense and you can prove it by the window, so go ahead and look."

Sam did, and saw what you see. What do you think he should do next?

Questions

1. Does Knut's story give him an adequate case of self-defense?

2. If your answer to the above is affirmative, would you nevertheless charge Knut with the illegal possession of a gun?

3. Do the bullet holes show which shot was fired first?

4. What action do you think Sam should take?

Solution on page 57.

Incident on the Ferry

It was one of those cold, blustery days just before Thanksgiving when people who own houses come to the island for the double purpose of celebrating the holiday and closing their houses for the winter. Among the crowd on the late Friday ferry were the McGlobs, Leander and Gilda. The next day, Gilda's body was washed ashore on an East Chop beach.

Sam, after a hard day's work interviewing several dozen people, got the following information:

Almost nobody knew the McGlobs, but a couple answering to their description had barely made the ferry in their car. The woman had jumped out of the car in a fury, yelling that she'd had enough of her husband's lousy driving and wasn't going to risk going aboard with him. She then ran to the stairway, at the top of which a man was apparently waiting for her. He embraced her passionately, and they boarded the ferry together. She was not seen again, but a few people noticed him and said he was alone.

The next day, McGlob appeared shocked when Sam informed him that his wife's body had been discovered on the beach. He admitted quarreling with her but claimed they'd had dozens of fights and the one on the ferry had been mild.

"You shoulda seen us when we really got going," he said with considerable pride.

"Spare me the honor and just tell me what happened," Sam said.

McGlob stated that he'd driven aboard the ferry and had been directed to a spot too near the wall for him to open his door. While he was protesting, a small station wagon was ordered to park alongside him, but so close that he was completely boxed in.

"Well, I raised hell. But what could I do, stuck in there? I took a nap, and forty-five minutes later when my wife didn't show up, I figured she was still mad at me, so I drove off."

McGlob was still being interrogated when a man named Sigmond Floyd walked into the Edgartown police station and said he was the man who'd embraced Gilda on the gangway.

"I'm her cousin and I hadn't seen her in a whole year," he said, "so naturally I gave her a big healthy buss. After that, she went out on deck."

McGlob, when told about Floyd, said, "Some cousin!"

If you were Sam, what would you do on the basis of these statements?

Questions

1. Is it believable that Gilda went out on the cold, windy outside deck?

2. Could McGlob slip out of one of the car doors and then proceed to find Gilda?

3. Could McGlob have climbed from his open window to the roof of the wagon?

4. If McGlob had left his car, would he necessarily have been seen and identified?

5. On the face of it, is there any evidence to substantiate either Floyd's story or McGlob's?

6. If you were Sam, what item of evidence would you look for on the basis of which to make an arrest, and whom would you charge?

Solution on page 58.

The Possible Dreams Auction

Anyone who has been on the Vineyard in August is familiar with the benefit auction called "Possible Dreams," with Art Buchwald as the auctioneer. It is held outdoors next to the pool in the courtyard of the Harborside Inn, where several hundred people attend and bid for such things as dinner for six at the home of a *New York Times* executive, a portrait to be painted by the local artist Jules Worthington, or an afternoon at police headquarters with Sam.

At the last auction, it became apparent that a couple in the balcony surrounding the courtyard were feuding with each other. The climax was reached in a bidding war that found the woman offering $8,000 for an afternoon on a mystery yacht rumored to be owned by a TV celebrity. The man abruptly gave up bidding and left her holding the bag at an inflated price. After that, the comedy was over and both left the balcony.

Gradually, the news rippled through the courtyard that the pair were the former Ken Shoemans, recently divorced and now remarried—he to a notorious former Miss America and she to a tenor named Fargo Farabelli. As fate would have it, the two couples were housed in adjoining suites that fronted on the long circular balcony.

After the tension subsided, the audience concentrated on Art Buchwald's auctioneering. As a result, no one was looking up when a man went tumbling down over the balcony.

Sam was the first to rush over and see the knife still protruding from the man's chest. After a futile attempt to help the dying man, Sam got down to business.

The murder weapon was a fruit knife of the kind that the hotel supplied, and a half-eaten apple was still clutched in the victim's hand. Meanwhile, a dozen people were yelling out their identification of the man: "Ken Shoeman, billionaire." With that, it was easy to narrow the investigation down to three suspects, shown here. They were:

Brenda Farabelli (C), the former Mrs. Shoeman, who said she and her husband had been lying on the couch near their door, talking about the auction, when they heard the commotion in the courtyard.

Fargo Farabelli (B), who backed up his wife's statement in every detail.

Sheila Shoeman (A), now a brand-new widow, who said she'd been resting after the excitement of the auction. Her beloved Kenny, meanwhile, had picked up an apple and a fruit knife and went out to the balcony, remarking that he wanted to enjoy his fruit with some scenery.

Sam listened, studied the three people, and made an arrest. Whom did he charge, and why?

Questions

1. Is it credible that no one saw who stabbed Shoeman?

2. Is it believable that Shoeman, if stabbed in his own room, staggered out to the balcony, where he fell?

3. Is there evidence that Sheila lied in her statement?

4. Is there evidence that Farabelli lied?

5. Is there evidence that Brenda lied?

6. Who killed Kenneth Shoeman?

Solution on page 59.

The Cruise of the
Good Ship Contessa

That the notorious Wanda Waring was bewitching is known, but that she bewitched the well-known Boston jewelers Deluz and Delai into lending her a half-million-dollar diamond bracelet, which she told them would be bought by Count Nixia del Amore, was somewhat surprising. Still, neither Deluz nor Delai was naive enough to entrust her with an uninsured bracelet, and if Wanda tried to pull a fast one, they were sure to be protected.

No one was surprised when the Count invited Wanda to cruise on his yacht *Contessa* and put her in the stateroom next to his, but a few eyebrows were raised when she brought along her eight-year-old daughter, Trixie. The Count's cruises were no place for a child, and after Trixie discovered she could throw things overboard and watch the splash, she became a terror.

When the boat docked at the Edgartown wharf for a few hours, the Count met Sam and invited him on an overnight cruise. Flattered, Sam dashed off to Brickman's and bought a yachtsman's cap. He was wearing it at sea the next morning, enjoying the brisk salt air with the Count and Wanda, when suddenly he heard a young girl giggling. Sam turned quickly to see what you see in the picture.

What did Sam notice, and what conclusions did he reach?

Questions

1. Does Trixie looked pleased?

2. Does Wanda look angry?

3. Is Trixie agile?

4. Was Trixie interested in seeing the splash?

5. What do you think Sam concluded from what he saw, and what did he do about it?

Solution on page 59.

THE AWESOME TREASURE

As kids, they'd always summered at Uncle Victor's, in the great, rambling mansion overlooking Edgartown harbor and the island of Chappaquiddick. The three kids used to play a game they called "Uncle Victor's Awesome Treasure," and the idea was to pretend they were expert harpooners and sail off in a whaling ship, but instead of killing whales, they would find a box of pirate gold.

But that was far away and long ago, and now they were grown up—she a professor of political science, her brothers, a doctor and an engineer. They hadn't seen Uncle Victor in years, but he'd summoned them one weekend in June. At the small Vineyard airport they were met by Bessie Sassado, who was Uncle Victor's housekeeper and perhaps something more.

Bessie told them that their uncle wasn't well, that all he did now was count his money. He kept a lot of it in a safe, in the little room with the stairs leading up to the widow's walk. Bessie didn't think he'd live much longer.

Just before dinner, Victor gave them a quick look inside his safe. They glanced at the stacks of money and certificates, and he told them he was going to make one of them his sole heir and that they were here so that he could look them over and decide who was worthy.

The next morning, Bessie came running down the stairs and screamed out, "The marster's been kilt—oh lordy me—come help!" Which all three did, and they saw what you see.

The doctor, after a brief examination, pronounced Uncle Victor dead, the result of a fractured skull. The doctor then called the police. Sam arrived promptly with Officer Pudge Bartlett and Bartlett's seven-year-old boy, Scoop.

Sam asked a few sharp questions and, together with Pudge, made an exhaustive search of the premises, with negative results. Meanwhile, Scoop was prying into every nook and cranny that he could find, usually with harmless effect, until he found a hammer, after which he went wild. He started with a table in the new gazebo and was banging up the floor when, by accident, he struck a loose plank. It turned out to be a trapdoor that covered a hidden compartment. With a yell, he shrieked "Look what I found!" and scattered a package of fifty-dollar bills.

If you were Sam, what would you conclude, and whom would you arrest?

Questions

1. Had Uncle Victor been killed accidentally?

2. Had he been killed during the course of a burglary?

3. Had the safe been ransacked before he was killed?

4. Who killed Uncle Victor?

Solution on page 60.

Vineyard Gothic

When Jupiter Kling inherited the Oak Bluffs property shown here, he looked it over and said he'd have to sell it, but first he'd make it a perfect house, ready for anyone to walk in and feel at home.

Two weeks later, he showed before-and-after photographs, reproduced here as drawings, and asked a few friends to list all the changes they could find.

Several people, including Sam, made perfect scores, but after examining the sketches, he said, "Fine, but there's one thing you forgot to do."

What was it? How would you make the house perfect?

Solution on page 61.

A CASE OF KIPPERS

Sara Palfrey loved kippered herring and had bought a dozen cans of it at Cronig's Market. She had them with her when she went to clean Casper Pollux's apartment in West Tisbury, as she did every Tuesday, but somehow or other she left them there and forgot all about them until Thursday. Since she had a key to Casper's apartment, she let herself in, only to find a body on the couch. Obviously strangled.

Not having read any mystery novels, Sara failed to scream. All she did was give a small gasp that nobody heard except herself. Then, as she said, she did a little straightening up.

"I like to see things neat," she said, "and she lying there with her dress sopping wet and an old garbage bag with a hole in it on her lap—I couldn't stand it."

After neatly folding the garbage bag and placing it over the arm of the sofa, she called the police and then sat down and opened a can of kippers. She munched contentedly while she stared at the body of Q. T. "Cutie" Buxom (who was neither cute nor buxom, but it was the first corpse Sara had ever seen, and she wanted to make the most of it).

Officer Milly Shooflu answered the call and shooed Sara out of the way. Sam, who had been in Lambert's Cove checking a case of vandalism, arrived as soon as he could. Within a couple of hours he had identified the body as Q.T.'s, learned that she was a loan shark, that Casper owed her $16,148.09, that last Tuesday he'd gone off-island on a business trip, and that according to the medical examiner, Q.T. had been strangled on Wednesday.

On the face of it, all Sam had to do was find Casper and charge him, but Sam was unable to locate him until Friday, when Casper walked in and expressed surprise at the murder. Since he could prove he'd been off-island on Wednesday, Sam was stymied.

As he always remarked, if you keep thinking hard enough, something happens, and it happened just after he'd passed the Flying Horses Carousel in Oak Bluffs and turned into Circuit Avenue, where he noticed Sara coming out of Mad Martha's with an ice cream cone of dripping Celestial Hash. That was when the idea struck him.

What was it, and how did it solve the mystery of the Case of the Kippered Herring?

Questions

1. Do you think that Q.T. came to Casper's to collect money?

2. Was Casper broke?

3. Did Casper have a motive for killing Q.T.?

4. What is the significance of the puddle?

5. What was Sam's idea, and how did it solve the case?

Solution on page 61.

THE $40,000 RAFFLE

The clambake, held on the Sengekontacket beach for the benefit of Vineyard Community Services, featured the raffle of a $40,000 car donated by Henry "Chip" Chandler to inaugurate his new car dealership.

The preparations were elaborate. Little Liz Kermooch, winner of the Chamber of Commerce Junior Spelling Bee, was to pick the winning number out of a chowder bowl while the audience waved Chip Chandler flags and stood around a bonfire. She was then to announce the number of the winning ticket, after which Chip was to set off some spectacular fireworks.

The sketch shows the scene as Little Liz is about to reach in to pick a number, a moment before the fireworks lit up the sky. However, before she could get her hand inside the chowder bowl, the heavy lectern with its bowl and contents was knocked into the fire, where it burned with a clear xanthene flame (due to the composition of the recycled paper). With that, Liz burst out crying, and Sam had his work cut out for him. He started by questioning the three people nearest the lectern.

The three, identified in the sketch as A, B, and C, are respectively Willy Tenwhistle, ballet dancer; Jack Torry, former Vineyard football star; and Chip himself.

Sam questioned the trio at length and then made a charge of Malicious Mischief and Intentional Destruction of Property.

Whom did he charge, and why?

Questions

1. Do you think Liz threw the lectern and tickets into the fire?

2. Do you think that one of the trio threw the lectern into the fire?

3. Who had a motive for destroying the tickets?

4. Do you think somebody could have been hired to destroy the tickets?

5. How do you think the lectern was knocked into the fire?

6. Whom did Sam arrest, and why?

Solution on page 62.

Over the Cliffs and Down We Go

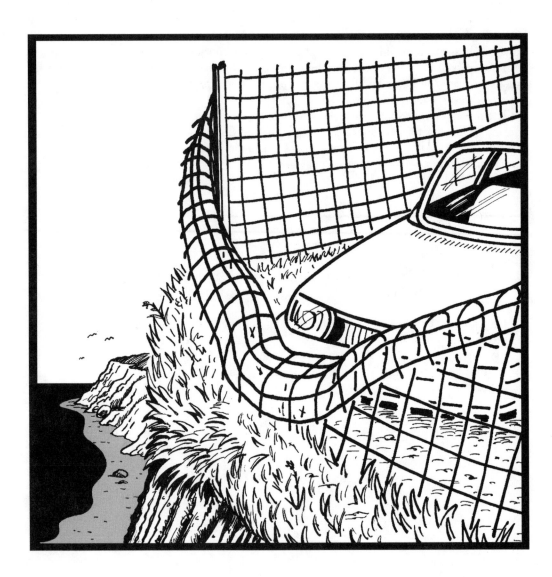

Sonny Day was far from sunny. As his wife, Dawn, pointed out, he was stupid, obese, obstinate, cantankerous, and had a ferocious temper, but he had one redeeming feature: he had money. Thanks to which she and her brother, Sherman Willingly, lived with Sonny comfortably and in apparent harmony until early one morning when a fisherman found Sonny's body lying face down on the beach below the Gay Head cliffs.

Sam, summoned before he'd even had breakfast, drove his jeep to the spot where the body had been found and made a preliminary inspection. It showed a badly bruised body, with bits of clay and twigs embedded in the clothing.

Leaving Officer Pudge Bartlett to guard the body, Sam made the long, circuitous trip from the beach to the top of the cliffs, where he saw what you see in the sketch. A half hour later, after a thorough investigation, he went to interview Sherman. He was breakfasting alone, and he showed more surprise than grief. Questioned, he stated that the Knights (August and June), who controlled Sonny's fortune as sole trustees, had been visiting last night, and after the second bottle of scotch, the conversation turned to finance.

In the middle of the discussion Sonny blew his top. In a sudden outburst he called Sherman a sponge and ordered him to get out of the house by morning. He then turned on the Knights, and told them he had evidence to prove they'd been embezzling and was going to present it to the D.A. the next morning. After a final diatribe against Dawn, he stormed out of the house and said he was going to the Gay Head cliffs where he could at least get some clean ocean air.

As Sherman finished his account, Dawn, only half awake, staggered into the dining room and said she'd heard what Shermy had said and it was God's honest truth. She then burst out crying and flung herself weeping on Sam's shoulder, soaking his shirt in tears. He waited her out and asked if he could go to the bathroom and wash up. She nodded sadly and said, "Please use the pink guest towel."

Sam cleaned up and drove to the Oak Bluffs Inn, where the Knights were staying. They corroborated Sherman's account of the drinking bout but stated that after Sonny's abrupt departure, Sherman had jumped up angrily and said, "Call me a sponge? I'll show you!" And he'd headed for the cliffs. The Knights, however, said they'd gone straight back to the inn.

Sam, faced with contradictory stories, sat down to think. What do you think he concluded, and what did he do about it?

Questions

1. Did Sonny fall to his death?

2. Was the fence damaged by the car?

3. Was it difficult to climb the fence?

4. Was the perpetrator under pressure to leave the scene?

5. Why do you think the fence was bent down to the ground?

6. Was this a one-man job?

7. Who killed Sonny?

Solution on page 62.

THE GREAT "DRUG" BUST

In fair weather, Sam likes to sit in the covered part of the Edgartown dock and munch a lunch with his friend Dippity Droop, who has an antique shop off Water Street in Edgartown. Although they both are jet-stream talkers, they say little because they're too busy observing the sights—kids fishing and the ferry crossing the narrow neck of the harbor to the island of Chappaquiddick.

Sam, who likes to look at antiques but never buys, went back to the shop with Dippity, whose nephew Pelvis Esley was minding the store.

Pelvis was full of excitement. "Somebody came in here," he said, "and walked straight to the back of the store, to that fifty-cent crockery sign, and then he stood there for a long time examining the stuff as if he knew what he wanted and knew it was there but had to locate it. Then he bent down and picked up a plate and studied it carefully. But instead of buying it, he put it down and stuck something underneath it."

"What?"

"I didn't look. I didn't want my fingerprints on anything because this looks like some kind of a drug deal and I don't want to get involved."

"Show me the plate," Sam said.

Pelvis pointed and Sam picked up the plate that was decorated with little angels who were shooting at each other with tiny pink bows and arrows. Then he picked up the folded piece of paper that had been underneath and unwrapped it. The gold locket that he uncovered was plain. When Sam opened it, there was a message inside that read, "Harbor View, 7 PM, #236."

Sam handed it to Dippity who examined it and said, "Locket's worth five hundred."

Sam replaced the plate and locket. "The guy say anything?"

"Oh, yes. He looked at me and said, 'What are you doing here?' Then without waiting for an answer he left. What do you think we should do?"

"Nothing," Sam said, "except wait."

The next day, according to Dippity, a tall woman lifted the plate, picked up the locket, and then bought not only the fifty-cent plate, but a Steve Lohman sculpture in wire showing a pair of lovers kissing. She bought it for $300 and paid for it in cash.

"Gives me an idea," Sam said.

What's yours, and what would you expect to find at the Harbor View?

Questions

1. Do you think the locket was placed under the plate in the course of a treasure hunt, the kind in which the players find clues directing them from place to place?

2. Do you think the woman came to Dippity Droop's for some specific purpose?

3. Was this a love tryst?

4. If you were Sam, what could you do?

Solution on page 63.

THE NIGHT OF THE CRABS

Summer jobs on the Vineyard are at a premium, but the catch is that when you get there, where do you sleep? With rentals out of reach of most seasonal salaries, a few men or women often band together and lease a house, and there are some strange combinations. Typical was this group of five—Jim, Ewald, Bo, Rudy, and Max—who rented a cottage last summer in Oak Bluffs.

They had little in common except inflated egos, which simmered most of the month but never got out of hand until Bo came back one afternoon with a bucket of large angry crabs, which he left on the kitchen floor before he went to work at the Harborside Hotel.

Since all five worked late, they'd established the custom of sitting around and having a few beers before going to sleep. On the night of the crabs, Ewald showed them a gun.

"I don't know whose it is," he said, "but I found it behind one of the books. Could have been lying there a long time." They passed the gun around and left it on the table when they decided to go to bed.

Jim was the first to turn in, but he bounced up with a yell and with a crab hanging on to his big toe. The incident brought a big laugh, until Rudy pulled back his bed covers and found another crab. Cursing, he sent it skimming across the floor, straight for Ewald's shoe. Ewald rescued the shoe and dashed off, but he tripped over the lamp cord, plunging the room into darkness. The result was a free-for-all that ended with a gunshot.

When the light was restored, Max had a wound in his foot and the gun was lying on the floor, as shown. Between his groans, Max accused Jim, who accused Rudy, who accused Bo, who called the police.

Sam, with Officer Nancy Nashawena, answered the call. After the usual preliminaries, he took each of the group into the next room and questioned them separately. They all denied ownership of the gun and denied using it.

Jim said, "It wasn't me. I was on the floor chasing one of those damn crabs." Rudy said, "Not me, I was finishing my beer." Bo said, "Not me. I was wrestling with Ewald, who was trying to choke me." Ewald said, "Not me, I wouldn't choke anybody. I had Bo by the neck because I thought he was a crab." And Max said, "Not me. Think I'd shoot myself?"

Under the circumstances, what do you think Sam did?

Questions

1. Did the bullet hit Max directly?

2. Describe the trajectory of the bullet.

3. Where was the perpetrator when he fired?

4. Who shot Max?

Solution on page 64.

Foxy Grandpa

For eight years, Grandpa Kilpatrick Daniel Kibbe and his three cats—named Underfoot One, Two, and Three—lived frugally on a boat moored in the harbor near the ferry landing in Vineyard Haven, but in the ninth year, he won a three-million-dollar lottery, and his life changed. He quickly sold his boat and bought three houses.

His favorite, which he called Mixed Blessings, was one of the gingerbread houses on New York Avenue in Oak Bluffs. There, sitting on its ornately flounced porch, he loved to sketch while he watched the boats in the harbor. His neighbors kept wondering what he was drawing. If they'd managed to peek, they would have seen Mixed Blessings drawn over and over again, compulsively, and always from the same angle. He even memorialized it in the document shown here, which he called his will.

His offspring—two married sons and a married daughter, plus a gaggle of grandchildren— forgave him his eccentricities. After all, with so much money he had a right to be a little different. But when he died and left his three houses mortgaged up to their roofs, plus an overdrawn bank account and the piece of paper shown here, they felt he'd carried things a little too far.

What do you think his progeny did, or should have done?

Questions

1. Could this be a holographic will, and as such, be valid?

2. Since the numbers are obviously some kind of code, would you expect it to be a simple one?

3. Try to solve the code, on the basis that it is a simple one.

4. What do you think Grandpa Kibbe's children did, or should do?

Solution on page 64.

AT THE FAIR

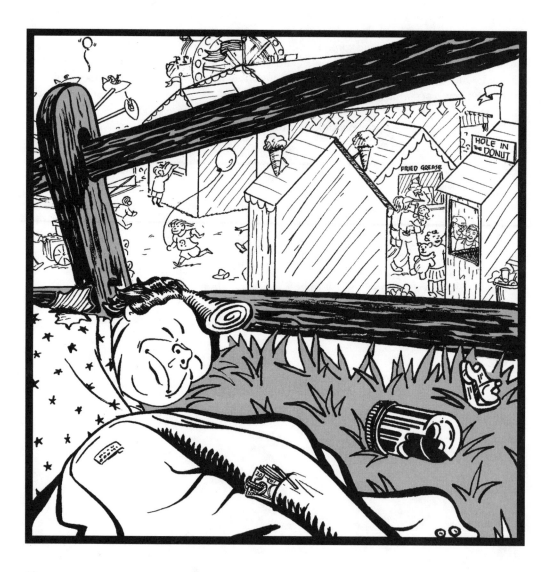

During the annual Martha's Vineyard Agricultural Fair, it never rains and the fair grounds in West Tisbury are bathed in a carnival atmosphere. Food booths, carousels, and a Ferris wheel crowd the midway, while the old Grange Hall bursts at the seams with competing exhibits of almost anything that can either grow or be made by hand, from quinces to quilts and artichokes to art. Not the least of all these entries is a Martha's Vineyard specialty—beach plum jelly.

Before her untimely death, Alice Tilton Freebooter's jellies had pulled in all the beach plum blue ribbons, but she would have been desolated to hear what had happened since. Because of the danger of botulism in home-prepared preserves, state regulations had prohibited actual tasting of any of the jellies. Instead, appearance—including color, clarity, and consistency—was now the only criterion for the award.

Colonel Freebooter, Alice's widower and a traditional head of the fair, was criticizing this procedure when he heard the shocking news that Scratchy Sonnenbaum, a second-rate carpenter, had won first prize for his beach plum entry. Worse than that, Sonnenbaum had insulted all the judges by grabbing his jar and blue ribbon and running off. The Colonel, aghast at this break with precedent and swearing to avenge the honor of the fair as well as the memory of his spouse, went looking for Scratchy.

Ten minutes later, Weary Willy, security officer for the fair, found Scratchy's body in the little-used area behind his wife Zinnia's "Hole in the Donut" snackery. On seeing what you see in the sketch, he called for Sam. Sam arrived forthwith, identified the body as Scratchy's, and cited a blow to the head as the cause of death. It took Sam only a few minutes to find out from some kids who had been playing nearby that, except for some of the booth-holders stepping out to deposit garbage, only two people had been in the area. Sam was able to prove that they were a pickpocket known as Fast-Finger Flanagan and the Colonel.

Sam studied the terrain carefully, and then on the basis of the above account plus what you see in the sketch, he decided who had killed Scratchy.

Questions

1. Had there been a fight?

2. Did the jelly jar break because it was dropped?

3. Why was no jelly spilled?

4. Why was Scratchy's money not taken?

5. What was the probable murder weapon?

6. Who killed Scratchy?

Solution on page 65.

SOLUTIONS

Solution to *Bang, Bang!* (page 2)

1. Yes. The wheelchair labeled MHV and the broken leg connect him to the J. Rolf who came to the hospital soon after the burglars had jumped off the balcony.

2. Either because of a quarrel over the loot, or else because his leg made him a marked man and therefore a constant danger to his accomplice.

3. Yes. If he'd been killed elsewhere, his body would have been left where it was, or else dumped in some remote spot.

4. To dispose of a body is always a problem. To leave it in a car or motel would lead quickly to the identity of the murderer. The killer must have decided that wheeling an apparent invalid to the park where the lighting was dim and where other wheelchairs would be would hardly arouse any suspicion. But for that errant cymbal, the ploy probably would have worked.

5. Sam reasoned that in the course of stripping the body, the killer noticed an almost full pack of cigarettes, and rather than waste it, he put it in his pocket. Since no one is likely to have two opened packs of different brands, each of which was opened in a different manner, it followed that one of the packs probably belonged to the victim. Sam therefore charged the owner of contents B with burglary, illegal transport of a body, and, to cap it all, homicide. Subsequent investigation confirmed Sam's quick diagnosis.
   Moral: Don't smoke.

Solution to *Windy Beach* (page 4)

1. No. He would not have brought a gun with him unless he expected danger, and if he'd expected danger, he would not have come to the rendezvous alone. Therefore, the gun must have belonged to either Ecclestrip or Soothsayer.

2. Yes. Despite the fact that Terwilliger was a gullible person and probably of less-than-sound judgment, he had excellent grounds on which to claim fraud.

3. No. Ecclestrip was far too smart to leave a dead body on his private beach. The presence of the small boat indicates that he might have planned to kill Terwilliger and then dump the body far out at sea. Whatever the original scheme was, Sam's

51

appearance when Ecclestrip had a corpse on his hands must have frightened him, and he therefore made up the story of the accidental shooting.

4. The soft sand showed where people had walked, but the prints were far too messy to point to any specific individual.

5. Ecclestrip. Sam had seen someone locked in a fatal embrace, and when Ecclestrip and Soothsayer accused each other of the apparent murder, Sam studied the marks next to the body. They must have been made by Terwilliger's killer, who had fallen with him and then managed to get up. Sam realized that a man of twenty-two would spring up easily, whereas an older man such as Ecclestrip would have trouble getting up and would need to use his hands and knees, and the hand and knee prints show clearly. Sam therefore accused Ecclestrip.

Suzie, thankful that she wasn't involved, told Sam that Soothsayer and Ecclestrip had planned to assault Terwilliger and then take him out in a boat and drop his body overboard. Terwilliger, however, had been too strong, and the gun that Ecclestrip happened to have with him went off.

"Accidentally," Suzie said. "The poor dear would never harm anybody."

"Except," Sam said, "Terwilliger." And Suzie shook her head sadly.

Solution to *Stradegy* (page 6)

1. Yes, judging by the broken furniture and other damaged objects.

2. No. Anyone owning a Strad would defend it with his very life and never risk damaging it.

3. Yes, in all probability.

4. No. The bits of tape used to mend cracks and other damage must have been applied before the fight. It follows that the Strad had been damaged previously and therefore was worth far less than the amount stated in the policy.

5. Belle. Sam asked himself the questions posed in numbers 2 through 4. The answers suggested that Belle had been faced with a worthless husband and a worthless Strad. Add the fact that an insurance man would lower the value of the Pagachini nest egg because of the damage and she was faced with a pair of problems that could be resolved with one big bust—namely the bronze Beethoven. As for his hand, Belle placed it there as a red herring to show her husband's affection for his beloved Strad. Her scheme, however, failed when Sam realized that she was the only person with the twin opportunities of killing Paggy and smashing the Strad. The only thing she was successful at was a good job of ululating, which she kept up all the way to jail.

Solution to The Peek-a-Boo Girl (page 8)

1. Yes. Nobody was bothering to come to his exhibit.

2. Yes. The Field Gallery was getting all the publicity and all the business.

3. Yes. Risky, but perfectly feasible.

4. Yes. As experts, they might well have been quietly discussing the extent of the damage and whether it was reparable.

5. No. Sam's search would be thorough and professional.

6. He accused Fanny because there was neither knife, letter opener, nor scissors in her drawer, one of which would be absolutely necessary in a gallery that often had to wrap pictures and open packages. Rather than getting her off the hook, the absence of scissors or a knife was fatal to Fanny, who could so easily have slashed the picture before opening the gallery and then blamed someone who had just come in—which is precisely what she did. Sam then searched Fanny and found the missing scissors.

"I hated that picture and decided somebody had to do something about it and I had such a wonderful plan. Then Sam had to go and spoil it. What does he know about art, anyway?"

Sam's friends rose to his defense, and he was asked to be one of the judges at the next All-Island Art Show.

Solution to *Tread Lightly* (page 10)

1. Probably. Her possession of the $800 in twenty-dollar bills, coupled with Sperling's withdrawal of the same amount, is almost conclusive. Add the facts of her marauding, and it seems likely that instead of sweets she found an interesting document, and used it.

2. No. Noah had no alibi, the others were self-serving and lacked any outside corroboration.

3. Yes. It is *prima facie* evidence and needs to be rebutted or explained.

4. It tends to clear him because, if guilty, he would probably have destroyed the shoe, or at least tried to prevent Sam from finding it.

5. The twins, on a charge of murder and conspiracy to commit murder. Sam was suspicious of the prints from the moment he first saw them because they were random impressions with no evidence of a walking pattern. Although Abel's shoe print was suspicious, he would have had to use crutches while walking on a narrow plank. The absence of any such marks cleared him.

As for Noah, although he was not Sam's favorite character, Sam could not imagine a father trying to frame his son for murder, but a pair of twins plotting against a brother is believable and has excellent precedents in the Bible. Sam's guess was that the twins knelt on the plank while one or both of them, with his hand inside Abel's shoe, pressed it down firmly. Their mistake was in underestimating Sam—a mistake they now regret, and will continue to for the next twenty years.

Sam regards this as one of his most important cases because it introduced him to the world of mushrooms. He is now an expert on *Agaricus arvensis,* which thrives on the Vineyard and which he eats with relish. Under Melissa's guidance, of course.

Solution to *A Matter of Delicacy* (page 12)

1. No, in each sketch there are eight dishes piled on the sideboard.

2. No, there are eight duplicate items in the two sketches.

3. Things changed:

   A. Sideboard moved
   B. Water level in pitcher lower
   C. Fruit missing
   D. Picture tilted
   E. Chair shifted
   F. Candlestick moved
   G. Glass moved

4. No, nothing seems to be missing.

5. Willy said "Bugged," because he noticed that the portrait had been moved slightly. Aware of the importance of privacy in the coming meeting, he decided the room had been bugged. He therefore looked behind the portrait, found the bug, and removed it.

   I'm sure you'll be glad to know that the minister and the ambassador came to terms, thus obviating a small but costly war, and proving that the atmosphere of the Vineyard is calm, serene, and a factor in world peace.

Solution to *In All That Rain* (page 14)

1. No. If he'd gone for a walk in the rain, he would have had suitable clothes, and certainly not gone in slippers and T-shirt.

2. Because Harry had not used it, and therefore could not have driven to the spot where his body was found.

3. No. If Harry had gone to Sackett's, Harry would have paid the money and taken back the IOU. Sackett's possession of it indicates that he probably never saw Harry on the day of his death.

4. Since Harry was drunk, didn't drive his car, and was still in slippers, it follows that he must have been carried out of the house and driven to the dirt road, where he was dumped face-down, with his head in the puddle, and left to drown.

Since one person could not have done all of the above, and since the last place Harry was known to have been was his own home, it follows that Elsbeth and Jughead must have gotten Harry drunk, taken his money, and then driven him to the lonely road where they murdered him.

Sam called this the most heinous crime ever committed on the island, although he admitted that the future might bring worse.

Solution to *Of Ghouls and Goblins* (page 16)

1. Yes.

2. Yes, but not without being noticed by the child in the chair on either side. Besides, the sound of the shot would have been deafening to anyone next to it.

3. He noticed the two jack-in-the-boxes, both of which had been sprung. One had the cloth figure still standing in the box, the other was empty. Sam realized that the box with the lid open would have been noticed. It followed that someone must have been able to coil up inside and then spring the lid and shoot

Meany. With everyone in the hall temporarily blinded, a revolver shot would be lost in all the confusion. Sam therefore went to Meany's office and looked for someone who could have coiled up inside the box. Lady Jacqueline Osgood, contortionist, answered the description.

4. Sam charged Lady Osgood with the crime.

At the trial, when the judge asked her to show how she'd been able to fit herself into such a small box, she drew herself up to her full five-feet-one-inch stature and said, "When I curl up like that, I expect to get paid!"

Solution to *Casey at the Plate* (page 18)

1. Yes. Any one of them—angry, perhaps drunk, and certainly frustrated—might well have gone berserk.

2. No. Under the circumstances, it is hard to believe that she'd expose herself to the rioters.

3. No, or at least highly unlikely.

4. No, it looks neat and undisturbed, except for the presence of a corpse.

5. There is no hard evidence against either Sports, Slippery, Twinky, or Eric, except that they were on the second floor at the time of the murder. As for I. M. Fair, the evidence against him is highly incriminating. He not only left The Lady alone in the hotel room, he also had no intention of returning. This is evident because her clothes are hanging in the closet, and he apparently took all of his, including his mask and highly cumbersome chest protector. Add the fact that he took an incredible risk by climbing down the rain spout, as opposed to staying in the safety of a locked room from which he could call the police if necessary, and it follows that he must have killed The Lady and then packed up and left.

At the trial, he refused to take the stand, and after the guilty verdict came, he was pestered by the press to make some kind of statement. He did so, angrily:

"The Lady claimed Casey was safe," he said, "and we got into one hell of an argument and I got mad because nobody can call me dishonest, not even The Lady. I call 'em the way I get paid to, so I said Casey was out and that makes him out. No question about it."

6. The umpire.

Solution to *A Comedy of Errors* (page 20)

1. Wrong leaf on tree.

2. Paint color is different.

3. Painter is wearing mismatched socks.

4. Ladder rung is not attached.

5. Painter casts no shadow.

6. The window latch is outside.

7. Two different curtain patterns.

8. Pants cuffs are different.

9. Cat has a lion's tail.

10. "I" in "Painting" is missing.

11. Painter has two right hands.

12. Painter is not holding can in the center; paint would spill out.

13. Nobody, especially a pro, would ever stand on the top rung.

Solution to *Missy Takes a Walk* (page 22)

1. It must have been thrown, since it is almost impossible for someone to have reached up and slung it over the branch. Furthermore, its position proves that it must have been thrown from the right-hand side of the creek.

2. They, too, must have been thrown from the right-hand side, since they landed on the left side at the bottom of the embankment.

3. On the right-hand side, as indicated by the above answers.

4. On the right, because if she'd been alive, she never would have permitted anyone to throw her equipment across the stream, particularly her precious camera.

5. The way all bridges break—if they do so—either from old age or from too much weight.

6. She must have been carried, which was obviously quite a feat.

7. Ricco, the out-of-work fireman. He was trained to carry people under difficult circumstances and was therefore able to carry Missy's body across the bridge and up to the top of the embankment.

    Under Sam's relentless questioning, Ricco finally broke down. "That picture she took of me when she was a rookie photographer at *The Tulsa Picayune*—it sent me up for five years. What business was it of hers if I set that little building on fire? There're plenty more, aren't there? Haven't been able to get a decent job since. So when I saw her all vulnerable and alone on that trail, I . . . well, I figured if I hid the body, nobody'd ever connect me with it. But no matter what happens, I want the boys back home to know I upheld the honor of Platoon Seven and that they ought to be proud of how I got her across that board. Shows what good training I got."

Solution to *Buck Shot* (page 24)

1. Yes. If true, his life was in danger and he had a right to fire back in order to protect himself.

2. Yes. Unless licensed, no one has the right to carry a firearm.

3. Yes.

4. He should arrest Knut for murder, because bullet B, which killed Buck, was fired first, and by Knut. This is proved by the fact that the lines radiating from

bullet hole A are cut off by those from bullet hole B. Therefore, the entrance bullet, B, must have been fired first. It follows that Buck was killed instantly and could not have fired. To set up an alibi, Knut must have gotten into Buck's car and fired Buck's gun through the window.

Smart fella, that Knut. But Sam was smarter.

Solution to *Incident on the Ferry* (page 26)

1. Yes. She'd had a nasty quarrel with her husband and went off in a huff. Feeling sorry for herself, she needed to be alone for a while.

2. No. Opening a door in an inches-wide space leaves little room in which to squeeze through.

3. Yes. It would not be easy, but it could be done.

4. No. McGlob knew only a few people, and most of the crowd had had a long trip getting to the ferry and were either too tired to notice much or else were busy chatting with friends whom they hadn't seen since summer.

5. No.

6. If McGlob had in fact climbed to the roof of the wagon, he would have left incriminating palm and finger prints.

Sam, finding them, would have a strong case against McGlob, and did. Besides the fact that he was the only person with a motive.

McGlob, faced with Sam's accusation, said, "All right. I climbed out. So what?"

"So you sneaked back. You might still have climbed out over the roof of the wagon, but if you'd been innocent you'd have had no need for an alibi, and you'd have waited for the wagon to drive off before going through the acrobatics of squeezing through your car window all over again."

After three hours of questioning, McGlob finally broke down.

"Okay," he said. "You got me. I climbed out of my car like you said and I went looking for Gilda, who was out on the open deck. When she claimed the guy she'd kissed was her cousin, I got mad and called her a liar and hit her too hard, and she fell overboard. And you know what? He really was her cousin!"

Solution to *The Possible Dreams Auction* (page 28)

1. Yes. In the excitement of the auction, no one would bother looking up at the balcony.

2. Yes, it is quite possible.

3. No, there is no reason to believe that she lied.

4. Yes. His half-shaven face is inconsistent with his claim that he was lying on the couch, talking to his wife. Some unexpected event must have happened to cause him to neglect the right-hand side of his face. Consequently, he must have lied.

5. If Farabelli lied, then Brenda no longer has an alibi. Since it's unbelievable that Farabelli would interrupt his shaving to go out and commit a murder, and since there is no reason to disbelieve Sheila, it follows that Brenda must have killed her former husband. Having done it, she rushed back into the room while Fargo was in the middle of shaving. Naturally, he didn't finish the job.

6. Brenda. On the basis of the theory outlined in answer 5, everything fits into place. While Farabelli was shaving, Brenda stepped outside. Shoeman, who had just publicly humiliated her, was calmly peeling an apple. The sight was too much for her, and she simply grabbed the knife and struck. She then rushed back to the room, where Farabelli stopped shaving in order to calm her down. Their hastily invented alibi might have stood up, but for the evidence of his unshaven cheek.

   At the trial, she pleaded self-defense. "I thought he was going to attack me," she said, "and I had to protect myself."

   The jury felt that a man who was in the middle of eating an apple was hardly a serious threat and convicted her of homicide.

   Under the circumstances, she was unable to spend an afternoon on the mystery yacht, but neither was anyone else, since it turned out to be owned by Kenneth Shoeman, former philanthropist.

Solution to *The Cruise of the Good Ship* Contessa (page 30)

1. Yes. You bet she does.

2. No, she seems proud of her child.

3. Yes, very. To grab the bracelet and run off without being caught, and then to toss it while running at full gallop is far more than an ordinary child is capable of.

4. No, she's not even looking at the sea.

59

5. Since Trixie's right hand is clenched and her left appears to be throwing something overboard, Sam wondered what was thrown, if anything. Having gotten that far, he sensed a scam in which Trixie's right fist was concealing the bracelet. Later, she'd turn it over to her mother. Wanda would then report the loss of the bracelet and sell it at leisure, a diamond at a time, while Deluz and Delai collected the full amount of the insurance.

Sam waited a few hours before accusing Wanda, in private. She pointed out that he had no proof and couldn't possibly have any until—and unless—he had the bracelet. Furthermore, he had no jurisdiction on the high seas.

Sam admitted the force of her argument, but said he could have her arrested on a charge of attempted fraud the moment she set foot on land. After thinking it over, she handed him the bracelet.

The following week, he brought it to Deluz and Delai. They thanked him and told him it was hardly worth the trouble of coming all the way from the Vineyard, since the bracelet was merely a piece of junk jewelry. Did he really think they'd trust Wanda with something worth a half million?

Which left Sam wondering what to do with the bracelet.

If you were Sam, what would *you* do?

Solution to *The Awesome Treasure* (page 32)

1. No, judging by the position of the body in front of the safe and by the bookend, which is too far from the body to have been knocked down accidentally by Uncle Victor's fall.

2. Yes, because the cash in the safe is missing.

3. Yes, because the safe could not have been opened while the body was blocking the door.

4. Bessie, because she was the only one of the four people in the house who could know about the trapdoor in the gazebo, which had been built only recently. For motive, Bessie had probably expected to inherit at least a large part of the estate, but last night she had learned she was getting none of it. Realizing that if she didn't grab what she could right now, there'd be nothing to grab. So she killed him after he'd opened the safe to count his money during the night.

Sam had no trouble getting a confession. "It was his own fault," Bessie said angrily. "I told him he ought to marry me, and if he had, I'd have waited for him to die. Served the old coot right, is what I say. And if I ever lay hands on that Bartlett kid, I'll put the curse of Beelzebub on him. Just you wait and see!"

A threat, however, that she had no chance to execute.

Solution to *Vineyard Gothic* (page 34)

The changes:

1. Stone chimney became brick

2. Missing eave ornament replaced

3. Extra trim added to upstairs door

4. Rocking chair on balcony repaired

5. Missing balustrade post replaced

6. Extra detail trim on stoop posts

7. Broken window replaced

8. Flowers planted

9. Porch flooring replaced

After considerable discussion and after some people claimed to have found some nonexistent changes, Sam said, "That's all fine and I commend you, but there's something none of you noticed. It's not what was changed, but what wasn't. You see, there's no keyhole in the door and you can't lock the house." Did you notice?

Solution to *A Case of Kippers* (page 36)

1. Yes, most likely.

2. Yes, judging by the bareness of the apartment.

3. Yes, he had a $16,148.09 motive.

4. It indicates that the garbage bag had sprung a leak and had probably contained water.

5. Sam was struck with the realization that if ice cream melts, so does ice, and if the bag had been filled with ice, the melting ice would not only account for Q.T.'s wet dress, it also would seriously alter some of the signs by which time of death is normally judged, such as the rate of cooling of the body, its color, rate of decay, and so forth.

Once Sam had guessed that the bag had contained ice, it was easy to theorize that Q.T. had come to collect a debt that Casper couldn't pay, that they'd had an argument, and that he'd strangled her. In order to alter the evidence determining the time of death, he "iced" her so he could set the time of death on a day when he was off-island. He expected to return in plenty of time to remove the bag and its contents, but his scheme backfired when Sara came into the apartment and called the police.

Casper, interviewed by the press, was livid. "Drat!" he exclaimed. "I got kippered!"

Solution to *The $40,000 Raffle* (page 38)

1. No. A child would have neither the strength nor the ability to carry out such an action.

2. To pick up such a heavy lectern while holding a flag in one hand—and do it unobserved—would be impossible.

3. Chip. With the winning ticket lost, he had all the publicity he could want, but no longer had to contribute a car.

4. Sure, why not?

5. The lectern must have been kicked into the flames, the tickets on top destroyed.

6. Not Chip, a small man who was not in a good position to kick the lectern. And not Tenwhistle, because a ballet dancer would never risk breaking a toe while kicking a heavy object and would probably have kicked straight up, rather than forward, since his training was to kick high. Therefore, Sam arrested Torry because as a punter he had the strength and the know-how to kick hard and with a forward motion.

   Under the pressure of Sam's interrogation, in which he relied heavily on Torry's vanity and reputation as a punter (he hoped to play professionally), Torry admitted that he was paid to kick the lectern into the fire.

   "And what a kick that was!" he exclaimed.

Solution to *Over the Cliffs and Down We Go* (page 40)

1. Yes, judging by the twigs and clay embedded in his clothing.

2. No. It would have been too risky to ram the fence and chance going over the edge. Also, the damage to the fence would have caused damage to the fender. It follows that the fence must have been pulled down intentionally, then the car moved there later to make it look as if it had hit the fence and stopped just in time.

3. No. The average person could have managed it.

4. No. At night, the area is deserted. The perpetrator had ample time in which to set up whatever scenario he or she chose, apparently choosing to make it appear that Sonny had rammed the fence and then, groggy from the accident, fallen down the cliff.

5. It must have been trampled down in order to lug a heavy object over the fence.

6. No. Had it been one person, the fence would have been bent more or less in a V-shape from the point of pressure.

The shape of the damaged fence, however, indicates that two people pushed it down from two points about eight feet apart.

7. The Knights, as indicated by answer 6. They felt they had to get rid of Sonny before he went to the D.A. the next morning. Once Sonny was out of the way, they figured they'd have time to cover up their embezzlement, or at worst make a deal with the D.A.

    As for Sherman and Dawn, they had no urgent need to kill Sonny. They had a comfortable living, and they were certain that tomorrow Sonny would be back and be sober enough to discuss matters sensibly.

    On the basis of Sam's reasoning and after an investigation, including fingerprints and other forensic evidence, the Knights were charged with homicide and eventually convicted.

    Dawn was jubilant. "Lucky me!" she exclaimed. "I get all his money and didn't even have to kill him!"

Solution to *The Great "Drug" Bust* (page 42)

1. No, because an expensive locket was left where any participant could easily have taken and kept it.

2. Yes. Why else would she have come to this particular shop and gone straight to the plates and the wire sculpture?

3. Probably. The expensive locket, the hotel rendezvous, and the fact that no one except this one woman came for the message argue for a pair of lovers arranging a meeting.

4. A difficult question to answer, since you're barging in on a very private affair, but I can tell you what Sam did. Having decided that this was a tryst, he sent a bottle of champagne to be delivered to room 236, Harbor View, a little after 7 P.M. Checking up later on, he found out that the delivery man from Al's Package Store had had to wait almost five minutes before the door was opened by a tall morose man wearing a dressing gown.

    The clerk at the Harbor View told Sam that 236 had been reserved under the name Smith, and that when the occupant checked out the next morning, the clerk recognized him as a selectman from one of the six towns.

    He was accompanied by his wife.

Solution to *The Night of the Crabs* (page 44)

1. No. The dent on the bureau, shown by the arrow, proves that it must have ricocheted before hitting Max. Its velocity was thereby reduced.

2. The bullet, which hit the bureau at about a foot above the floor and then hit Max at about the same height, must have traveled on a horizontal plane of about the same elevation.

3. In view of the above, the perpetrator must have been on the floor.

4. Jim, who not only admitted being on the floor but offered the incredible alibi that he was chasing a crab in the dark.

    After Sam broke the alibi, Jim admitted firing the shot and owning the gun.

    "With my reformatory record, I was afraid of what would happen if I got found with a gun. There was no place to lock things up, so I figured the only safe place in the room was behind the books over there, and then Ewald went and found it anyways. When the lights went out, I grabbed it—it was mine, anyhow—and I went looking for that big crab that bit me. When I heard it moving in the dark with nobody anywheres near it, I took a pot shot. I guess I missed. And if that bullet hadn't ricocheted, everything would have been all right.

    "But it's Ewald's fault in the first place—why in hell would he want to go and read a book?"

    For an answer, Sam charged Jim with third-degree assault, illegal possession of a weapon, and the willful discharge of a dangerous weapon.

    As for Ewald, Sam held that reading a book was not a criminal offense.

Solution to *Foxy Grandpa* (page 46)

1. Yes. A holograph is an instrument written entirely in the hand of the person who appears to have signed it. Under this definition, the document under consideration can qualify as a holographic will.

2. Yes. Grandpa Kibbe was a simple man and would be expected to use the simplest and best-known code, namely the substitution of the number 1 for the letter A, 2 for B, and so on for the rest of the alphabet. Try it.

3. On the basis of the above, the will will read: *Take care of my cats.*

4. Since the will seemed frivolous and since Kibbe had apparently died without any money, his sons and daughter got together and moaned, until the brightest of the bunch (the girl, of course)

remarked that the state never pays out the full sum of a large lottery winning. Rather, it pays in twenty equal installments. Grandpa, having won $3 million, was being paid $150,000 per year, and with twelve years to go, each of his heirs could count on $50,000 per year for the next twelve years.

They were the best-cared-for cats on the island.

Solution to *At the Fair* (page 48)

1. Yes. You don't get hit over the head hard enough to kill you without some kind of a fight.

2. No. The jar would not break merely because it had been dropped on the soft, grassy surface.

3. Because there was no jelly in the jar. Although the jar had been broken and was lying on its side, nothing trickled out. It follows that the jar must have contained some kind of hard substance. Subsequently, Sam found out that the jar had been filled with a tinted plastic—exactly the color of beach plum jelly—and the plastic had hardened in the jar.

4. Obviously, neither Zinnia nor the Colonel would have robbed a corpse, but Fast-Finger would have been delighted to. Since Scratchy's money is still on his person, it follows that robbery was not the motive and Fast-Finger is no longer a likely suspect.

5. The jelly jar, with its plastic filling, constitutes a good solid weapon. No other weapon is visible.

6. The Colonel. He came with fire in his eyes, determined to examine the jar and find out why Scratchy had run off with it. The confrontation resulted in the fight in which Scratchy was killed.

   At the trial, the Colonel pleaded guilty and, because of extenuating circumstances, received a sentence of only three years. When the Colonel was let out of prison two years later for good behavior, a delegation of Martha's Vineyard housewives met him and presented him with six jars of beach plum jelly. He keeps them on the mantel above his fireplace, next to a portrait of his wife.

   He has never opened them.

Lawrence Treat, the author of many mystery novels and countless short stories, is past president and a former director of the Mystery Writers of America, of which he was one of the founders. He received the Edgar Allan Poe award in 1965 for the Best Short Mystery of the Year, and a second Edgar in 1978 for editing the *Mystery Writers' Handbook*. He was a prizewinner at the Crime Writers' International short story contest held in Stockholm in 1981, and he received a special Edgar Allan Poe award in 1986 for his TV story on the Alfred Hitchcock program. This is his eighth pictorial mystery puzzle book, a form he originated. He lives on Martha's Vineyard with his artist wife, Rose. Larry and Rose are hiding in another picture in this book. Can you find them?